Dear Parent:
Your child's love *of reading star*

fferent v
etween
thers re
reader in ....me more
her own interests and abilities. From
the first books he or she reads
alone, there are I Can Read Books for every stage of reading:

SHARED READING
Basic language, word repetition, and whimsical illustrations,
ideal for sharing with your emergent reader

BEGINNING READING
Short sentences, familiar words, and simple concepts
for children eager to read on their own

READING WITH HELP
Engaging stories, longer sentences, and language play
for developing readers

READING ALONE
Complex plots, challenging vocabulary, and high-interest topics
for the independent reader

ADVANCED READING
Short paragraphs, chapters, and exciting themes
for the perfect bridge to chapter books

I Can Read Books have introduced children to the joy of reading
since 1957. Featuring award-winning authors and illustrators and a
fabulous cast of beloved characters, I Can Read Books set the
standard for beginning readers.

A lifetime of discovery begins with the magical words **"I Can Read!"**

Visit www.icanread.com for information
on enriching your child's reading experience.

To Luke, who loves Halloween
almost as much as dinosaurs.
—K.G.

To my daughter, to encourage her
to taste pumpkin pies!
—O.V.

HarperCollins
PUBLISHERS

I Can Read Book® is a trademark of HarperCollins Publishers.

Library of Congress Control Number: 2016939341
ISBN 978-0-06-235315-3 (hardcover) — 978-0-06-235314-6 (pbk.)

17 18 19 20 21 SCP 10 9 8 7 6 5 4 3 2 1 ❖ First Edition

I Can Read!

SHARED My First READING

DUCK, DUCK, DINOSAUR

PERFECT PUMPKIN

Written by Kallie George

Illustrated by Oriol Vidal

HARPER
An Imprint of HarperCollinsPublishers

This is Feather.

This is Flap.

4

And this is their brother, Spike.

It is fall.

Time for picking pumpkins.

"I will find a perfect pumpkin," says Feather.

"Me too! Me too!" says Flap.

"PERFECT?" says Spike.

"Start looking," says Mama.

They look.

Up and down.

All around.

"I found a pumpkin," says Feather.

"It is perfect for . . ."

"JUMPING!" says Spike.

SQUISH!

"No, Spike! Not perfect for *jumping*," says Feather.

"Not jumping! Not jumping!" says Flap.

"It's okay," says Mama. "Keep looking."

They look.

In and out.

All about.

16

"I found a pumpkin!

I found a pumpkin!" says Flap.

"It is perfect for . . ."

"BOWLING!" says Spike.

SQUISH!

"No, Spike! Not perfect for *bowling*!" says Feather.

"Not bowling! Not bowling!" says Flap.

"It's okay," says Mama.

"Keep looking."

They look.

Left to right.

Out of sight.

"We found pumpkins!"

say Feather and Flap.

"They are perfect for . . ."

"JUGGLING!" says Spike.

SQUISH!!!

"No, Spike!" says Feather.

"Pumpkins aren't perfect for juggling.

Or bowling.

Or jumping."

"They are perfect for decorating!"
says Feather.

"See," says Feather.

"See, see," says Flap.

Spike does see.

He sees squished pumpkins.

"Cheer up, Spike," says Mama.

"Squished pumpkins are perfect too."

"Perfect for pumpkin pie."

"YUM!"

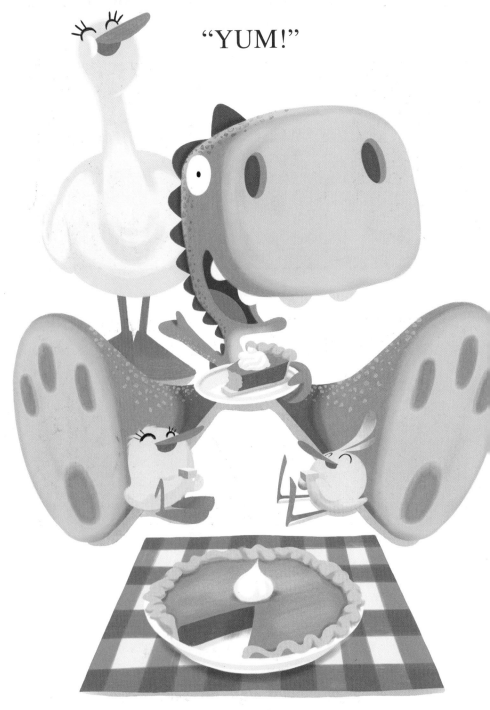